The Conflict Resolution Library™

Dealing with Lying

• Lisa K. Adams •

The Rosen Publishing Group's
PowerKids Press™
New York

Published in 1997 by The Rosen Publishing Group, Inc.
29 East 21st Street, New York, NY 10010

First Edition

Book Design: Erin McKenna

Photo Credits: Cover by Olga M. Vega; all other photos by Seth Dinnerman.

Adams, Lisa K.
    Dealing with lying / by Lisa K. Adams.
        p.   cm. — (The conflict resolution library)
    Includes index.
    Summary: Explains what lying is and why people do it; then discusses trust, living responsibly, and the value of telling the truth.
    ISBN 0-8239-5071-9
    1. Truthfulness and falsehood—Juvenile literature. 2. Deception—Juvenile literature. 3. Honesty—Juvenile literature. [1. Honesty.]
    I. Title. II. Series.
BJ1421.A33 1997
177'.3—dc21
                                                97-4146
                                                  CIP
                                                  AC

Manufactured in the United States of America

Contents

What Is a Lie?

A lie is saying something that you know is not true. Sometimes people lie because they are **embarrassed** (em-BAYR-est) to tell the truth. Other times, people lie because they are trying to trick someone.

Just about everyone has told a lie at some time in their lives. Just because you have lied before does not mean you are a terrible person. But it does mean you might have made a bad decision.

◀ Sometimes people lie because they want people to think that they are better than they are.

Why Do People Lie?

People have many different reasons for lying. Some people lie to make themselves look better. If a student gets a bad grade on a test, she might lie to her parents or friends and tell them that she got an A. A boy who does not want to share his candy might lie by telling his sister he has no more candy.

Have you ever lied about something bad that you did because you didn't want anyone to find out about it?

A person may lie to a friend because he wants to keep something all for himself. ▶

Lies Damage Trust

Trust (TRUST) is when you are sure that someone will not let you down. It is one of the most special things you can have with other people. When you trust someone, you know he will not hurt you or lie to you. But when a person lies to someone who trusts him, the trust is **damaged** (DAM-ejd).

If your best friend told you a lie, how would you feel about him? You might stop trusting your friend. Then it might be hard to be friends.

◀ People may stop trusting someone
who lies to them.

Grandma's Favorite Mug

One day, Lisa broke the handle off her grandmother's favorite mug by mistake. Instead of telling the truth, Lisa hid the broken mug in the hall closet. When Grandma asked Lisa what happened to her mug, Lisa lied and said she didn't know.

Grandma found the mug later. But Lisa's lying upset Grandma much more than the broken mug did. It took a few days for Grandma to feel as though she could trust Lisa again.

Telling the truth is much better than trying to hide it from someone. ▶

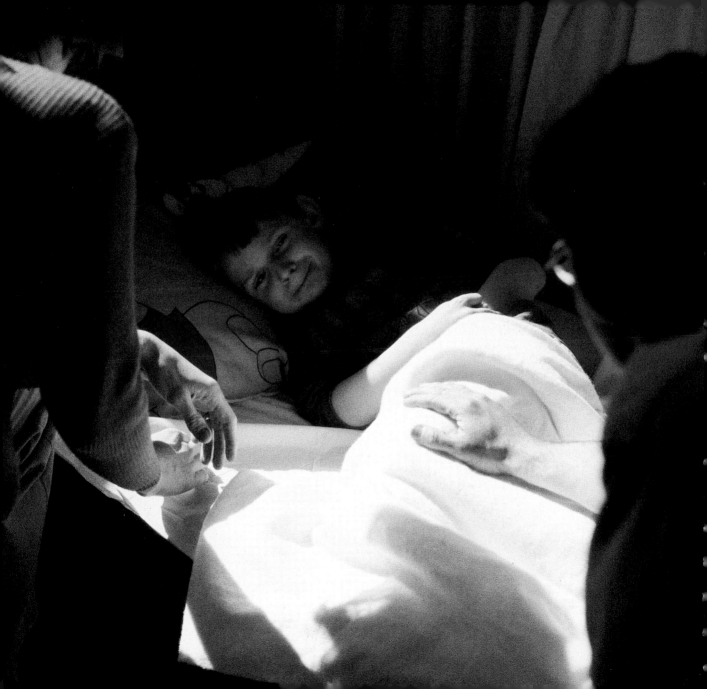

Lies Can Be Dangerous

Terry's parents told him never to take anything from their medicine cabinet. But Terry was curious about some pretty pink pills inside. One day, Terry ate some of them and they made him very sick.

His parents asked him what was wrong. At first Terry lied and said he didn't know. This was very **dangerous** (DAYN-jer-us). Terry's parents couldn't tell the doctor why he was sick. But luckily Terry told the doctor. Terry's lie could have put him in danger.

◄ Telling the truth can also be important for your safety.

13

Lying For a Friend

Sometimes a friend might ask you to lie for her. But lying for someone else could get you into big trouble. If your friend asks you to lie for her, ask if you can help her in another way. Tell her that telling the truth is better than lying.

All friends make mistakes from time to time. But remember, a real friend will not make you choose between lying for her or losing her as a friend.

Some friends need to understand that it's wrong to ask someone to lie for them. ▶

White Lies

Have you ever heard of a **white lie** (WYT LY)? A white lie is a lie that is often told with good **intentions** (in-TEN-shunz).

Friday was Jan's birthday. Her mom came to Jan's classroom after lunch. Jan asked if she had brought cupcakes for the class to celebrate her birthday. Jan's mom said no, but she held something behind her back. Jan's mom told a white lie because she didn't want to ruin Jan's birthday surprise.

◀ Sometimes people tell white lies to avoid hurting somebody's feelings or ruining a surprise.

Exaggeration

Sometimes people **exaggerate** (egg-ZA-jer-ayt), or stretch the truth a little bit. They don't mean to deceive anyone. But they want to make a point.

Mark was telling his best friend about a visit to his aunt's house in Wisconsin. He said, "It was so cold, I nearly froze to death!" Mark didn't lie, but he did exaggerate the truth. He wanted to make the point that he was very cold.

Exaggeration can make a person's story ▶ sound scarier or funnier than it really is.

Living Without Lying

The best way to avoid lying is to stay out of situations where you might have to lie.

Katie's library books were overdue. When she finally turned them in, she almost lied and told the librarian that she couldn't return the books because she had been sick. But Katie knew she would feel even worse if she lied. Instead, she apologized for taking so long to return the books. Katie knew that if she had returned them on time, she wouldn't have felt bad in the first place.

◀ The next time you feel like lying, ask yourself whether it's worth it or not.

Make Yourself Proud

The worst part about telling a lie is that it can make you feel **ashamed** (uh-SHAYMD) or bad about yourself. Lying can hurt you on the inside.

Telling the truth can be hard. But being honest, even if you might get punished for it, is worth it. Chances are, others will **admire** (ad-MYR) you for not lying. You'll feel proud that you were brave enough to tell the truth.

Glossary

admire (ad-MYR) To like and respect someone or something.

ashamed (uh-SHAYMD) To feel guilty or bad about something.

damaged (DAM-ejd) To have harmed or have hurt.

dangerous (DAYN-jer-us) Able to cause harm.

embarrassed (em-BAYR-est) To have made someone feel uncomfortable.

exaggerate (eg-ZA-juh-rayt) To stretch beyond the truth.

intentions (in-TEN-shunz) Reasons why you do something.

trust (TRUST) Knowing that you can count on someone to be honest and to care for you.

white lie (WYT LY) A lie that is told with good intentions.

Index